"My friends passed it around for about 2 hours during the Super Bowl! They loved it . . . I couldn't believe it, those guys don't read anything!"

Kyle Ryan, University of Toledo

"I'm a junior at Brown University and I picked up the book on a whim for my brother who's a senior in high school. I read through it and was amazed at how true the title is. It really is just about everything I should've known before I left for college . . . if my brother absorbs even half of it, he's going to have it ten times easier than I did."

Lance Nathan, Brown University

" . . . I could not believe how inspiring, helpful, and accurate this book was. I've read it from cover to cover more than once . . . it's made college so much less of a mystery."

Reynold Duclass, R.A., University of Miami

"... a wonderful book ... so realistic it almost scares me."

John Dalton, Assistant Dean of Student Affairs, University of Florida

"It's like having your best friend say, 'I'm gonna tell you exactly what you need to know.' Every college student should read this."

Dr. Meladee McCartny, Educator, 'Chicken Soup for the Soul (A 4th Course)'

"This book is an integral part of our orientation program ... I tell students and parents that the seminar is worth the price just for the book alone."

Don Willis, Associate Dean of Students, Missouri Western State College

"It is some of the best college advice we've read ... many thanks for providing such an honest and worthwhile book."

Carol Elfring, Novi Community School Board

BEEN THERE *Should've* DONE THAT

∧

More Tips for Making the Most of College

2nd Edition

SUZETTE TYLER

FRONT PORCH PRESS
HASLETT, MICHIGAN
OUACHITA TECHNICAL COLLEGE

BEEN THERE Should've DONE THAT II

Copyright © 1997, 2001 by Front Porch Press
Written by Suzette Tyler
Cover by b.j. Graphics
Cover photography by Doug Elbinger
Design by Jeff Fillion

Excerpt from Levitz/Noel National Dropout Study, 1991, by permission of USA Group, Noel/Levitz, Iowa City Iowa. Some quotes have been edited for clarity and brevity.
Any references to registered trademarks incorporated herein are purely coincidental. These references are not made for the purpose of drawing upon the goodwill and intrinsic value of such trademarks.

Published by Front Porch Press, P.O. Box 234, Haslett, Michigan 48840
Phone: (517) 487-9295. Fax (517) 487-0888. E-mail: styler@voyager.net

ISBN 0-9656086-1-1
Library of Congress Catalog Card Number: 96-62016
Printed in USA

ACKNOWLEDGMENTS

I am immensely grateful to the many young people who shared their thoughts and experiences. It's their voices that give this book meaning. My sincere appreciation also goes to:

- A very dedicated staff in the University Undergraduate Division at Michigan State University.

- Bob Scriver, Jay and Francie Todd for their technical advice and patience.

- Jennifer Braselton, Kim Broviac, Karen and Terry Casey, Andrea and Mike Cirrito, Andrea Funkhouser, Frances Kaneene, Laura Luptowski, Linda Newman, Janet Robison, Kendra Shipps, Lisa Scriver, Diane Wanagat, Jeff Wolcott, and Nell Wolcott.

- Judy Eyde and Sarah Gilin for their photographic skills.

- Misty Johanson, Aaron Newman, and Lisa Reinhart, my interviewers.

- Pat Sladek, Carol Potter and Gail Dunham for their great encouragement.

- Gary Tyler for his unwavering support despite dirty laundry and an empty refrigerator . . . even *before* the book.

- Adam and Josh Tyler, whose trials and errors inspired me to be a better adviser and mom.

CONTENTS

INTRODUCTION

We're back with Been There, II! It's filled with more wonderful insight from students and recent grads across the country. We've also included in this edition, advice from 'the horse's mouth' . . . the professors themselves. Let there be no question what it is they want in a student! While I'm no longer doing college advising in the formal sense, I'm still privy to the continuing "should'ves" and "could'ves" of college life via the many students I talk with while traveling. As ever, their revelations . . . and confessions . . . contain advice that is refreshingly insightful and encompassing. Clearly, collegians everywhere encounter similar challenges. With a little editing here and there, their advice is as comprehensive and "expert" as it gets. The following pages will help campus newcomers, as well as veterans, discover how to make the most of their college years—sooner, rather than later. My thanks to all who shared their wisdom.

S. Tyler

The problem with college is that you figure it out about the time you're ready to graduate.

Senior, Economics, University of Florida

"I was pretty busy concentrating on my social life during orientation and welcome week. Attending information sessions definitely wasn't a priority. Unfortunately, I missed a few 'key points' that might have made life a little easier . . . like the admissions requirements to the college of business."

Junior, Communications, Michigan State University

The 'Orientation' Express

To Do's . . . and To Don'ts

Pick an early session. I waited until late in the summer so I could go to orientation with a friend. Forget that! All the courses were closed.

Sophomore, Advertising, University of Florida

I felt like 'odd-man-out' the first semester. Everyone knew everyone— *except me.* New freshmen had been invited to spend a week during the summer doing a community service project. I didn't go.

Junior, Economics, Duke University

Don't blow off welcome week programs. Learning about majors and campus activities or how to use the library sounds pretty dull, but it's the ONLY time most of that stuff is offered. It's a quick, painless way to get a lot of information. *GO!*

Senior, Telecommunications, Michigan State University

Get rid of a course you're dreading by taking it at a community college during the summer before classes start. I wish I had . . . my math course sucked up so much time during the first semester that I got crummy grades in everything.

Junior, Psychology, Southern Illinois University

Use a map to schedule classes. I didn't . . . and spent a semester running from one end of campus to the other.

Sophomore, Psychology, UCLA

During orientation, I found out who I needed to talk to about writing for the school newspaper and contacted them. By the time recruiting meetings were held several weeks into the fall semester, **I was already an 'old-timer'** on the staff.

Junior, Journalism, University of Michigan

A guaranteed JUMP-START

Had my mom not twisted my arm to take a freshman seminar, I wouldn't have. She was right . . . it gave me a huge jump-start. I learned what it took to do college-level work, research majors, and find all these incredible things on campus that I would otherwise never know existed. In fact, I'm amazed at how many of my friends, as seniors, still don't know they do.

Senior, Communications, Appalachian State University

All that mail you start getting once you're accepted... **READ IT!** Colleges put extra dollars, faculty, and advisers into programs to help freshmen succeed... *but you have to enroll in them!*—The Adviser

My roommate and about 30 other kids on the floor were all in a really cool program while I, having paid no attention to the information about special freshmen programs, spent most of the year feeling lost.

Sophomore, Michigan State University

Course/program names differ on each campus—i.e., Freshman Seminar, Learning Communities, FIG-Freshman Interest Group, Mentoring Programs, etc. Ask an adviser. (There is often limited space available.)

Book Smarts

Buy your books during orientation. If you wait until fall, the lines will be *humongous* and there won't be any used books left to buy.

Junior, Architecture, University of Michigan

Keep your receipts! The text might change or you may decide to drop the class.

Graduate, Biology, Columbia University

It sounded a little 'anal' at the time but a friend of mine found out what the assigned reading was for his English course and read the book during the summer. Probably that wasn't such a bad idea.

Junior, Economics, SUNY/Stony Brook

Note: Most bookstores allow you to reserve books via their website.

Placement Tests . . . DON'T GUESS!!!

I must have been psychic when I took the placement tests. I guessed at everything and ended up in classes that were over my head . . . *BIG MISTAKE!!!*

Junior, Environmental Science, Indiana University

Note: If there's a chance you can "place out" of a requirement and placement results are "suggested" rather than mandatory—guess away.

"I was like 'this room is a *single* . . . right?'
WROOONG!

Sophomore, Engineering, Notre Dame

Dorm Details

Martha Stewart . . . NOT!

My plan for decorating our room was awesome—matching comforters, **white-eyelet pillows, window valances, and periwinkle blue carpet.** My roommate's plan was based on a Pell Grant, the Stafford Loan, and a comforter from home. I quickly ditched the Martha Stewart stuff. Our room looks fine, and we get along great.

Sophomore, Nursing, University of Michigan

Moving In Musts

"Pay the extra fee to move in a day early. When the cars are lined up and the elevator's jammed, you'll be glad you did."

"If you're the first to move in, don't grab the best bed, desk, dresser, and closet. It won't impress your new roommate."

"Report *any* room damage *before* you move in so that you won't be charged for it at the end of the year."

"Don't try to save bucks buying a used rug unless it's *really* clean. Old rugs are killers if you have allergies."

"Don't pound nails in anything without permission."

Housing—Options and Opinions

'Quiet floors' are the way to go. You can always study in your own room and screw around on another floor. *DePaul University*

Community bathrooms are great. There's no waiting when you *need* to use it, no conflict over whose turn it is to clean it and it's a great place to hear what's happening . . . plus that's where I practice my speeches. *University of Illinois*

Substance-free dorms are just a lot of people having fun without all the garbage that comes with drinking. *Wake Forest*

Single rooms are okay for sophomores, but not freshmen. It's harder to meet people and there's no one to go to dinner with. *University of Michigan*

All-girl dorms are great. Girls make better friends when guys aren't around. *Marquette University*

MAKING BIG, small . . .

I'm in a "living/learning" dorm—everyone lives in the same dorm and most of our classes are together. I was worried that it might get old real fast, but it's been great. My friends who aren't in this program spend day after day in huge lectures and never see anyone they know. I know everyone, including the faculty. **It's like a small college with Big Ten sports.**

Sophomore, Lyman Briggs College, Michigan State University

Dorm dining . . . food for thought

"Get it out of your mind that you have 'to get your money's worth.'"

I ate and ate and ate. I'd tell myself, 'just one cookie.' So I'd have one cookie, a brownie and a sundae. By midterms I had to lay on the bed to zip up my pants.

Junior, Economics, Northwestern University

There are great restaurants in this town and they all deliver to the dorms. I couldn't figure out where all my money had gone the first few semesters, until I realized I'd eaten it!

Junior, Nursing, University of Michigan

"You might not like dorm food but it's already paid for."

'Mystery Meal' Revenge

Bar Pizza
Pita bread or bagel (deli bar)
Marinara sauce (pasta bar)
Cheese (salad bar)
Veggies (salad bar)
Zap in microwave.

Grilled Cheese Sandwich
Toast two slices of bread
Snag some cheese (slices from deli bar or
grated from the salad bar)
Zap in microwave.

Steamed Veggies au Gratin
Veggies (salad bar) *Place in a bowl with
water. Cover with second bowl and ZAP.*
Cheese (salad bar) *Place in a bowl with
water to thin and ZAP. Pour over veggies.*

Baked Apples
Slice apples
Add cinnamon, sugar (optional: butter and
raisins)
Zap in microwave.

"Bring a zip-loc bag and grab veggies and cheese for your bookbag."

5, 10, 15 . . . 40!!!

The 'Freshman 15' isn't from dorm food. It's alcohol and ordering pizza when you're trashed at 3:00 A.M.

Junior, Business, Miami of Ohio

The 'Freshman 15' is more like '40'—you can't go anywhere without fast food or latte's staring you in the face.

Junior, English, Indiana University

To increase your metabolism eat within one hour of getting up.

Healthy U.

From little leagues, to middle school, to high school, I always played competitive sports. My biggest mistake was not taking time for it in college.

Graduate, Sociology, Purdue University

I like exercise when it's called something else—tennis, ice-skating, swing dance. The only way I'm consistent is if I enroll in a class where attendance is taken.

Sophomore, Psychology, University of Washington

I treat working out as a 4-credit class . . . one hour, four times a week. It's the best stress-reliever ever.

Junior, Journalism, University of Michigan

"Anywhere else you'd be paying for a health club—better work your butt off while it's free".

The apartment thing . . .

I couldn't wait to live in an apartment, but looking back, it was really more fun in the dorm. I met tons of people and there were more things to do . . . plus, the bathrooms were cleaner.

Graduate, Marketing, University of Wisconsin

"You lose a lot of time cooking, cleaning, driving back and forth . . . looking for a parking place!"

Don't move off campus until you have a base of friends. It's isolating.

Senior, Political Science, University of California, Santa Cruz

Live in the dorm for two years. When you move off campus you never hear about anything, whether it's good parties or good classes.

Senior, Economics, University of Connecticut

Once I moved out of the dorm, I was done. It's so easy not to go to class. **I never ate!** At least the dorm had meals. Plus, you need a car. That means gas and insurance!

Ex-Sophomore, Engineering, Central Michigan University

> **Face it!**
> **To live with *anyone* 24 hours a day**
> **in a room the size of a closet is**
> **gonna bring on some tense moments,**
> ***friend or not.***

Junior, Sociology, University of Colorado

Roommate Roulette

Luck of the draw . . .

I'm from Des Moines and pretty conservative . . . I took one look at this kid's posters, the clothes in his closet and his CD's and thought 'NO WAY.' That was four years ago and we're still roommates. It's been cool . . . and I've grown.

Senior, Business, University of Iowa

Every part of his body was pierced—*EVERY part*—and he loved to show *everyone*. Between that, the punk music he went nuts to, and the porno pics he also loved to show, it was a little tense. But looking back, it was only a few months out of my life and I have stories I can tell forever.

Sophomore, Undecided, Princeton University

"Going in Blind" . . . Pros and Cons

People aren't as considerate with friends as they are with strangers. It's easy to take advantage of one another and ruin a friendship. *University of Pennsylvania*

I had more problems with the roommate from home than the one who was a complete stranger. *Michigan State University*

Rooming with a friend gave me the confidence to meet more people and try more things. *St. Mary's College*

Go for it. If it works out, you've made a friend for life. If it doesn't, it's only temporary. Nothing ventured, nothing gained. *University of Colorado*

*MSU, 2000

Shhh . . . only 26% of students believe that it's wrong to share a secret with someone when asked not to.*

I roomed with a high school friend and we ended up barely speaking. I still had to go home to the same town where we both had the same friends . . . her mom knew my mom, her dad was my dad's client . . . **blah, blah, blah**. It wasn't worth it.

Junior, Business, Miami University

"Your best friend may be a slob, but it doesn't bother you until you have to live with it."

Alternatives . . .

My best friend and I requested the same dorm, but not the same room. It was great because we ended up having friends individually and together. If I needed a familiar face or wanted to get out of the room, there was always someplace to go.

Junior, Psychology, Southern Illinois University

I'm a wimp . . . I wouldn't have had the courage to go to an out-of-state college if my friend wasn't going too. We were roommates but we shared a suite with two other girls so it was kind of like having the best of both worlds.

Junior, English, Indiana University

So Bert and Ernie it's not . . .

I was raised with three brothers. My roommate was an only child. We drove each other nuts . . . but I actually missed her over the summer.

Sophomore, English, DePaul

Don't expect too much . . . your roommate won't necessarily be your best friend. That's okay.

Senior, Broadcasting, Marquette University

College is a good time to become the person you want to be. People accept you for who you are now, not who you were **in the third grade.**

Junior, Economics, Williams College

OUACHITA TECHNICAL COLLEGE

It bugs the hell out of you when your roommate's boyfriend is in the room ALL the time, even if he's a nice guy.

Senior, English, Aquinas College

Before It Gets *Ugly*

The 'R' word . . .

You don't have to hang out with him, you don't have to like him, but you do have to RESPECT him.

Junior, History, Notre Dame

I had an incredible roommate all four years. She was so easy to live with because before doing anything she always asked a question, "Do you mind if . . . ?"

Graduate, Engineering, Iowa State University

Cutting Through
THE BULL . . .

The biggest mistake that roommates make is that instead of just telling the other person what they're mad about, they do something to get even . . . so then everybody's mad and it just snowballs.

Junior (R.A.), Engineering, University of Miami

Compromise . . .

Take a break. My roommate studied constantly— *in the room!* It was like a monastery. We're all in college to study, but there are times you need to do it elsewhere.

Sophomore, Education, Vanderbilt University

My roommate had this "need" to make our room "Party Central" all hours of the day and night. I was too gutless to suggest anything as nerdy as "quiet hours." It lasted until grades came . . .. At least this nerd's still in school.

Junior, Geology, Arizona State University

The kid was *glued* to the Internet . . . that monitor light was *never* off. About three in the morning, I'd want to kill him!

Junior, Biology, University of Michigan

Borrowing boundaries . . .

Set limits. After letting my roommate borrow a sweater, my closet became a "free-for-all," especially if I left for the weekend. Make it clear that it's an "ask first" policy and set a specific time that you "need" it returned.

Senior, Psychology, Adelphi University

Clean it. Sharing clothes starts out as a great deal—until the sweater you were planning to wear smells like a gym bag or a brewery.

Senior, Business, Northern Illinois University

"What really ticked me off? He never shared the cookies that his mom sent!"

Know when to throw in the towel . . .

Don't drag it out. My first clue should have been the day I arrived and found the entire room rearranged and *my* desk in the hall! It was downhill from there. If it's bad to start with, it'll only get worse. There are usually a few "no show" spaces available in the fall. Request one.

Junior, Psychology, Southern Illinois University

or

Gut it out. It's just where you sleep. Spend time in other rooms and chalk the semester up as "an experience." It'll give you time to find a roommate you *do* like for the next semester.

Senior, Human Development, University of Connecticut

TOP 10 Ways To Make Your Roommate Happy

10 Buy your own shampoo and deodorant—*and* use it.

9 Wash your cereal bowl and socks *before* they're green and fuzzy.

8 Keep your wet towel off the beds

7 Keep visits from high school friends down to something less than a week.

6 Don't hit the "snooze" a thousand times for an eight o'clock you're not going to anyway.

5 Keep your beverages off the computer.

4 Don't erase the answering machine and then announce, "Someone called but I don't remember who . . .." Write it down.

3 Remember, it's a *dorm* room, not a romantic hideaway.

2 Don't disappear when it's time to pay for the pizza . . . or anything else.

1 **Flush.**

> **"I** went to preschool with the same kids I graduated from high school. I never had a moment of trying to figure out where I fit in— until college!**"**

Sophomore, Economics, Williams College

Bummers

I cried everyday for the first month. I couldn't even call home because I couldn't talk without sobbing. You just want to sit and do nothing . . . and that's the worst thing you can do. Force yourself to get busy.

Junior, Psychology, Southern Illinois University

The hardest thing to get used to is doing things alone. In high school I never even went to the bathroom alone much less *ate* alone. You have to learn to walk up to people and start talking.

Junior, Chemical Engineering, M.I.T.

Don't go home the first month. It only makes it harder when you come back. Besides, that's when everyone is anxious to make friends and there's a lot going on.

Junior, Engineering, Notre Dame

It's a bonding thing . . . friendships are made when you're hanging around doing nothing.

Junior, Social Work, Rutgers University

The best way to get over being homesick is not to go home.

Senior, Political Science, University of California, Santa Cruz

Long distance relationships are tough to pull off. The biggest mistake I made was having a girlfriend at another school the first two years. Neither of us really *enjoyed* college. It makes you older than you are.

Senior, English, Denison University

It was hard to go back after Christmas break my freshman year. I was still wondering whether I'd picked the right college. I'm glad I did. Any college is fine once you find your group of friends.

Sophomore, Economics, Williams College

"I was trying so hard to make friends that I wasn't me."

GimmeSpace...

There's no privacy in the dorms. The first year was like not being able to breathe. I eventually found a family off campus who needed a baby-sitter and it was like reconnecting with **the real world . . . kids, pets, houses.** They've become my family away from home. It's really a nice break from the dorm.

Sophomore, Physical Therapy, Northwestern College

"I just want real carpet and real food."

"It ain't easy being green . . ."

—Kermit the Frog

Here I was 1,000 miles from home dealing with people who had funny accents, tatoos, piercings, and sexual preferences I hadn't encountered before. Late-night talks in the girls bathroom opened all sorts of horizons . . . I realized that having a tongue ring did not make you scary—*that's quite a lot for a girl from Iowa.*

Graduate, English, Simon's Rock College of Bard

I felt like I was by myself as people on my floor started finding groups. I wasn't much of a drinker . . . and then, you always wonder if it's a race 'thing.' I was thinking of transferring. Then I joined a cycling club, somthing I love . . . and things just kinda fell into place. I'm glad I stayed.

Senior, History, Marquette University

I felt like I was the stupidest, poorest person on campus my freshman year.

Graduate, Bio-Psychology, University of Michigan

I was surrounded by kids who were phenomenal and *I* just wasn't getting it. I was doing everything I was supposed to and still flunking. **It wasn't until my sophomore year that I really felt like I fit in . . . that I could do it.** I had been just angry enough that I wasn't gonna let it beat me and that's what kept me going until I found classes that I loved.

Senior, Sociology, Harvard University

OUACHITA TECHNICAL COLLEGE

> **There's no reason to fail—NONE! There are people here to help and it's free. *Actually*, you've paid for it, every single thing, so you might as well use it.**
>
> *Senior, Education, Michigan State University*

I was 'the stuff' in high school. In college it was like "Whoa, this is the 'Pros' . . . I'll look *really* stupid going to the tutoring center." Eventually, it was obvious that what was really stupid was NOT going.

Graduate, Psychology, Spelman College

There were office hours after class every day, but nobody ever used them except me. It was like private tutoring.

Graduate, Management, Ferris State University

ADVISOR

HELP!

Learning Center. Determine your particular learning style and develop better test-taking, note-taking, and reading skills.

Writing Center/Help Rooms. Help is provided for writing papers and tutoring sessions are offered for specific subjects.

Mentoring. Students are 'connected' to a faculty member or an upper-classman who offers insight and encouragement on an informal basis.

Career Center. Assessment tests and counselors will help you clarify goals and examine appropriate careers/majors.

Counseling Center. Help is provided for personal concerns, anxiety, substance abuse, eating-disorders, sexual assualt and other issues.

> **I see kids get so hung up on grades that they miss everything else. College is more than a GPA.**
>
> Junior, Chemical Engineering, MIT

Note: 37% of students who drop out have GPAs of 2.5 or above. For reasons other than academics, they have not "connected" in the college setting. (Levitz & Noel National Dropout Study)

Carpe Diem, Definitely!

Seize the day!

The phone number on one little flyer that I noticed my freshman year just grew into a 'dream position' I've had all four years. The people I've met and the doors it's opened have been incredible.

Senior, Film Production, Penn State Univeristy

There's a lot of cool stuff on campus, but you have to look for it. I was so caught up in making friends and writing papers my freshman year, that college was no bigger than my dorm. I finally got involved in a campus group, and through that, a research project. I should have done it sooner.

Senior, Physiology, Michigan State University

All anyone wanted to talk about during job interviews was what I'd done *outside* of the class.

Graduate, Engineering, University of Michigan

READeverything!

Bulletin boards, the campus newspaper, mail—I
didn't pay much attention to any of it and I missed a
whole lot of things because I didn't . . .. **I could
have been scuba diving** in San Salvador for my
natural science requirement!

Graduate, Humanities, Michigan State University

The #1 misspelled word by college students? Definitely.

HELLOOO . .you're paying $23,000 a year for *more* than going to class and eating in the cafeteria.

Senior, History, Marquette University

I went from playing sports and being active in lots of other high school activities to doing pretty much nothing in college. It took me a while to realize that **you don't just sign up for stuff in 'homeroom'** ... you have to get off your butt and find it.

Junior, Social Work, Rutgers University

It was really cool to be able to wave at the president of the university and have him know who I was . . . Being active in campus groups introduced me to 'key' people and opened a lot of doors.

Graduate, Communications, Weber State University

A friend dragged me to a meeting . . . I'd never even heard of the group. It ended up being my focus in college! I've gained so many skills and so much confidence . . . more than in the classroom—*and it's been more fun.*

Junior, Business, University of Wisconsin

The smartest thing I ever did was to become involved in activities campus-wide, not just within my major. I didn't miss out on anything.

Senior, Music, Murray State University

> People are the best part. Having friends makes college easier.
>
> *Sophomore, Education, Vanderbilt University*

Sign up for dorm rep or join a committee . . . you'll get to plan the social events *AND get the funds to do it!* We did great stuff—trips into the city, "munchies" once a week. You meet tons of people and find out everything happening on campus!

Senior, Business, Northwestern University

The best part of college has been Swing Club . . . *yeah, as in dancing!* It gets me away from the 'grind' and I've become good friends with kids in other majors—it's a nice opportunity to get a different perspective.

Senior, History, Weber State University

Be a sport.

IM sports are a blast . . . you meet tons of people! Nobody takes it seriously. The only ones with actual "plays" are grad students and ROTC'ers . . . *kinda scary.*

Junior, Economics, Northwestern University

Don't overlook the obscure varsity or club sports . . . the perks are the same whether it's football or fencing. I've made great friends, traveled, *and I get to register early!* The team jackets, sweats and stuff are kind of impressive, too . . .

Junior, Michigan State University

Wherever you are . . . *BE there!*

If I had it to do over I'd have gone to more than just football games and parties. There were excellent speakers, concerts, theater *all right there!* Those things aren't available to me now . . . and for sure, *not at student prices!*

Graduate, Marketing, University of Wisconsin

I figured I might as well 'give it a shot.' I'd never even been in the high school choir let alone sung on stage until I got to college. Who would have thought I'd be auditioning for the Manhattan School of Music?

Senior, Education, Central Michigan University

GO GLOBAL!!!

I'd sell my car, my stereo, and everything I own to repeat the experience I had in an overseas study program! I learned more during that semester than all the rest put together.

Senior, English, Denison University

"It may be the only point in your life you'll have the time and your parent's money to do it."

Service-Learning . . . the real world

Volunteering in the community has not only allowed me to test my skills, but it reminds me why I'm in school. I can go six stops on the subway from Harvard Yard and I'm able to link classroom theory with real people. The change of pace keeps me sane.

Senior, Sociology Harvard University

I tutor math at a local grade school . . . it's like a mini-vacation for me. It gets me off campus and I don't have to think about school.

Senior, Engineering, MIT

Note: Community volunteer opportunities are available through 'Service-Learning' programs on most campuses.

"College keeps you in a bubble . . ."

Cancun . . . or Appalachia? Alternative Spring Breaks

Everyone came back with a tan. I came back with amazing stories of people that I had met at a shelter for political refugees. It was an awesome experience . . . an eye-opener. I learned so much about international politics and gained a real sense of my place in a very big world— *all in a week!*

Junior, Journalism, University of Michigan

"At least one spring break ought to be something other than endless drinking and spending money . . . "

www.breakaway@alternativebreaks.com

"Choosing courses can make or break you in college. The better you are at it, the better your grades and the less your aggravation."

Junior, Sociology, University of Colorado

Choosing Courses

In the beginning . . .

Even if you're Einstein, the first semester is a big adjustment. Don't get so hung up on getting out in four years that you bite off more than you can chew. You can always pick up extra credits somewhere along the line.

Junior, Labor Studies, Saint Joseph's University

A friend of mine had tons of Advanced Placement credits and ended up taking *all* upper level courses his first semester. He almost flunked out! **AP courses don't always prepare you for college work,** especially the pace. If he had mixed in a couple of beginning level courses or retaken an AP class or two at the college level, his GPA wouldn't have been obliterated.

Sophomore, Advertising, University of Florida

I was valedictorian in high school, so it was pretty discouraging when I had to work a whole lot harder— **for C's!** I should have started with an easier load and built up some confidence.

Sophomore, Premed, Cornell University

91% of freshmen expected to have a 3.0 or higher at the end of their first semester. (CIRP/MSU, 1999)

Balance Is Everything!

It's better to take fewer credits and do *well* than just *get by* with more. GPAs are too hard to bring up!

Junior, Human Development, University of Connecticut

The number of *courses* you take is more important than the number of *credits*. Four courses worth 16 credits are more manageable than five courses worth 15 credits.

Junior, Kinesiology, University of Michigan

Don't schedule too many heavy reading courses in the same semester, and *definitely* not more than one lab!

Sophomore, Premed, Cornell University

Quick Tips

"Continue a language immediately. If you wait until the second semester, everyone else will be coming off the first . . . very fluently."

"Take computer courses ASAP. Why wait . . . they're skills you can use throughout college."

"Don't let the title or course description fool you. Some of the worst classes *sound* fascinating."

"Be choosy. If a class or prof doesn't seem 'right,' change sections or drop it immediately while you can still get another class."

"Take electives. They'll help you decide on a major and make college more fun."

By-passing the beginning

I "C.L.E.P.'ed" out of some courses just by studying a textbook over the summer and taking the test. It allowed me to fit music classes into my schedule that I wouldn't have been able to take otherwise.

Graduate, Engineering, Iowa State University

Introductory 'survey' courses can be harder than upper-level courses because they cover more material. If you're a sophomore, try an upper-level course. The focus is narrower, the classes are smaller, and the profs are often better. Plus . . . **they seldom give less than a B– for fear they'll keep one of those whiny seniors out of law school.**

Junior, Journalism, University of Michigan

Note: There are C.L.E.P (College Level Exam Program) tests for most 100 level courses. Check to see whether your school accepts them.

'Weeder' Wackers

Avoid taking 'weeder' courses your first semester of college whenever possible. There are enough challenges as it is—you don't need one more.
Graduate, Bio-Psychology, University of Michigan

Take large lecture classes on the 'off' semester. Classes are smaller, you can find out who the good professors are, and the curve's not usually as high. My life would have been far less stressful if I had taken Chem 101 during my second semester.
Sophomore, Engineering, University of Pennsylvania

"Look for seminars and small classes."

From the grads . . .

Whatever your major, DON'T blow off writing courses. I'm an accountant and my whole job is WRITING! There's reports to my boss, reports to clients, memo's to the file, and you *never* leave voice mail messages—it'e-mail! *University of Michigan*

I'm an art major who really could've used some marketing and sales courses. Not *every* company has a "sales force." You're it . . . plus a lot of other things you didn't major in. *UCLA*

I use my communication course every day. It taught me how to confront people without alienating them and listen to customers and 'hear' what they're *really* saying. *Milwaukee School of Engineering*

. . . the courses you *REALLY* need

I'd rather be criticized in a classroom than a conference room. I avoid talking in front of a group at all costs. A public speaking course in college would have been a lot better place to get over the fear. *University of Michigan*

I always knew I wanted a career helping people. What I didn't realize was that if you reach any level of responsibility you'll be knee deep in figures and formulas. You *need* basic finance and accounting courses. *Boston College*

Every day's a 'group project' in the real world . . . nobody does their own job *'by themselves.'* A course in small group communication should be *mandatory. Weber State University*

It's now or never . . .

Man, there are *so many courses* I wish I'd taken in college. I always kind of thought I'd like broadcasting . . . so how is it I never even took a course in it? What a waste.

Graduate, Marketing, Ohio University

I wish I'd taken more courses outside my major. Everything I did—tutoring, summer jobs, whatever—was with children. All for my resumé, nothing for me..

Graduate, Education, Central Michigan University

The sailing course was an unbelievable experience! I'll probably never get a chance to take a class like that again in my lifetime!

Senior, Psychology, Michigan State University

I chose my classes based on what my friends were taking or who the "easy A" professor was. In retrospect, I wish I would have taken the classes I was interested in and focused on learning something that I cared about. The academic part of college would have been so much more exciting.

Graduate, Business, Notre Dame

Don't waste money on blowoff courses. **Take what you're really interested in.**

Junior, Engineering, Notre Dame

" **Pick the professor, *not* the time of day.** "

Junior, Economics, Duke University

The Perfect Schedule

I used to pore over the schedule book for hours trying to arrange the perfect schedule. **No way would I consider a class before 10:00 or after 2:00**, and definitely no Friday afternoons. I *never even looked* to see *who* was teaching the course. After getting 'hosed' on instructors a few times it finally occurred to me that my method might be flawed ....

Senior, Economics, University of Connecticut

A good professor can make the most boring course on campus fascinating . . . and vice-versa.

Senior, Economics, Carleton College

Nothing grinds you more than a friend having the same class with another instructor who's a lot more interesting . . . *and* less work. **You'll kick yourself for the whole term.**

Junior, Economics, Duke University

"When you find a great professor, take every course he teaches."

Know thyself . . .

I like eight o'clocks. I roll out of bed, throw on a sweatshirt and go. Then I can study in the afternoon when it's quieter, and have my evenings free.

Sophomore, Communications, John Carroll University

Eight o'clocks are the worst! Nobody goes to bed before 2 A.M. Ultimately, you end up sleep deprived and cutting class. Guaranteed.

Junior, Advertising, University of Florida

"Set the AM/PM mode correctly."

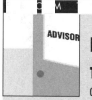

Know What You're Getting . . .

Talk to upperclassmen. Students often know better than advisers what courses and profs are best.

Check the bookstore for a book that rates the instructors.

Sit in on a class the term before or stand outside the classroom and talk to students as they come out.

Beware of empty seats. If the only section that's still open has lots of seats available and it's not an eight-o'clock, chances are there's a reason.

Read the syllabus. Borrow it or browse through it at the bookstore.

Make it easy on yourself

Register for an extra class.
After the first week or so, drop the course you like the least.

Sophomore, Psychology, UCLA

Schedule classes back to back.
You're less likely to cut.

Junior, Business, University of Alabama

Schedule two hours between classes and use it as 'built-in' study time.

Senior, Biology, Occidental College

The three-hour classes, one night a week are great! It's one night not wasted screwing around in the dorm, and the prof always lets you go early.

Senior, Marketing, Ohio University

Summer is a good time to take difficult courses. Instructors are more relaxed, classes are smaller, and the competition is less. It's perfect for taking labs.

Junior, Engineering, Notre Dame

Don't take "no" for an answer . . .

If a class will fill before my enrollment date, I find someone with an earlier enrollment and have them "hold" it for me. It takes a coordinated effort, but it's worth it.

Junior, Packaging, Michigan State University

It was closed but I went to the class every day, waiting for someone to drop. No one ever did, but the prof eventually took pity on me and let me in anyway.

Sophomore, Psychology, UCLA

If you can't get into a class, talk directly to the instructor. Say something to set yourself apart from the *other* 20 people who are trying to add it—mention a colleague who "suggested the class," talk about your "special interest" in his area . . . whatever it takes.

Senior, Marketing, Ohio University

"You are basically *screwed* if you miss a math class!"

Sophomore, Economics, Williams College

m..mm..mmm...MATH!

Famous Last Words

"Nobody collected the homework so I figured I'd just wait and do it later . . .."

"I didn't want to waste money taking the math I placed into, since I'd already had it in high school . . .."

"I couldn't understand the instructor so I decided to teach myself out of the book instead of wasting time in class . . .."

"Math was easy for me in high school and the first chapters covered stuff I knew, so I didn't actually *work* the problems . . .."

"It was just a bad day when I took the placement test so I enrolled in the next level . . .."

CALCULUS kills . . .

Even if you place into it, think twice before starting with calculus *unless* you've had it in high school. Most of the class has, and you'll be at a definite disadvantage if you haven't.

Junior, Economics, Duke University

Note: If that is the only math required by your major and a stellar grade isn't necessary, try it.

Solutions . . .

"Take math at a junior college. Classes are smaller."

"Don't buy a calculator without a backup battery."

"Do practice problems without looking at the answers first."

"Look for small classes. The seating capacity of each classroom is usually in the schedule book."

"You can't cram for math tests. It doesn't work. Keep up with the daily stuff so you won't have to."

"Math opens the door to some great majors. Hang in there."

T.A. tips . . .

Find a good one. Most math classes have a common final so it's important to get a good T.A.—*preferably one who helps write the final.* Ask around. If the department won't tell you which section a T.A. you want is teaching, call him and ask.

Sophomore, Engineering, University of Michigan

Change sections. If you can't understand a T.A., switch sections right away. But don't assume he's a bad teacher just because he has an accent.

Junior, Engineering, M.I.T.

Having a T.A. is like dating—find out what you have in common and then make the most of it. *University of Tennessee*

Regroup . . .

DO NOT, for *any* reason, go on to the next math level if you barely got through the first one. You'll get killed. Repeat the course.

Sophomore, Engineering, Central Michigan University

If you're lost after the first few weeks, drop back to a lower math. **I was beating my brains out** in calculus and barely getting a C. I dropped back to precalculus, got an A, and ended up getting an A+ the next semester in the same course that had been killing me before. I probably would have dropped out of engineering if I hadn't been able to fill the gap between high school and college math. It's a big jump.

Sophomore, Engineering, University of Michigan

The 'NEVER FAIL' Formula

***Before,* not after.** Doing assignments *before* lectures instead of *after* is the secret to math. I know exactly where I'm having trouble and what I need to learn.
Miami University

***Now,* not then.** Don't wait until you're totally lost to get help. See the instructor or get a tutor right away.
Western Michigan University

***All,* not some.** You have to be a maniac about math homework. Do *all* the problems.
Arizona State University

***Sooner,* not later.** No matter how well I understood things in class, if I waited a couple days to do the homework, I was lost. Do homework ASAP.
Albion College

"I was an expert at avoiding courses that required writing and at finding papers I could "borrow." Unfortunately, that made for some tense moments when I discovered how much writing was expected in my first real job. It would definitely have been smarter to have perfected that skill in college.

Graduate, Marketing, University of Wisconsin

The 'Write' Stuff

Foolproof fundamentals . . .

Make it easier on yourself. Choose a topic that you want to learn
more about . . . or research issues related to careers you're interested in.

Graduate, History, Howard University

Submit a rough draft. *ALWAYS* ask the T.A. or the professor to review
your rough draft before turning in the final paper. They're more likely
to grade a paper favorably if they've "helped" write it.

Sophomore, Art, Bowling Green University

Confirm your thesis. I put *hours* into a huge paper only to find out that
I'd done it wrong! DON'T write a word until the professor has approved
your thesis.

Junior, Business, University of Michigan

"The only 'A' paper I've ever written . . .

. . . was when I thought the due date was a week earlier than it was. It was amazing how many times I 'tweaked' it during that extra week."

Sophomore, Criminal Justice, Missouri Western State College

I try to revise every paper 3 times. When you start early it becomes like your 'baby' . . . if you're late, you just want to get it done.

Junior, Economics, Northwestern University

QUICK TIPS

"Pick a topic that can be used for more than one course."

"Pick a topic in which the professor isn't an expert."

"Make an outline."

"Proofread out loud."

"Don't plagiarize it. Cite it."

First impressions count . . .

A good-*looking* paper is huge with some professors . . . they're like 'OK, here's 10 points for extra effort.'

Senior, Business, Winthrup University

You need to set the mood. Make sure you're using the format your professor prefers—12 point type? Double-spaced? Margins? . . . *whatever!*

Sophomore, Undecided, Princeton University

"A MAJOR, MAJOR, MAJOR tip . . . make your introduction AWESOME!!!"

Research Papers

Online . . .

Before picking a topic, check the Internet . . . you don't want one where there's very little information available.

Senior, Economics, Notre Dame

Know the web address of journals in your field so that you can access the full text without going to the library.

Graduate, Microbiology, University of Michigan

. . . and off.

I can find better information, faster, at the library! Instead of spending hours sifting through websites I use the library's Help Desk. They know every conceivable resource and help you find it.

Junior, Business, Western Michigan University

*"The Internet makes it easier to plagiarize . . .
and easier to get caught."*

www.gotcha

As a member of the Student Conduct Committee, I've seen a lot of denials turn to excuses when we pull up the exact website that was copied. In the 'olden days,' instructors had only their suspicions when they came upon PhD-level work connected by 4th grade transitions. Now, it's like, **Hey, Slick, we've got some pretty damning evidence here!'**

Senior, Government, Franklin and Marshall College

" I'd like to go back to my freshman year . . .
get some good grades . . .
make more intelligent decisions . . .
I just didn't have a clue. "

Senior, Economics, University of Florida

Get a Clue

CLUE #1 Self-Discipline!

Dorm rooms are a setup for failure. You're surrounded by every distraction you can possibly think of.

Junior, Geology, Arizona State University

There's always *someone* who wants to do *something*. All I had to hear was, "Wanna hoop?" and I was gone. After grades came, I left my Nikes at home.

University of Toledo

Cable's a killer. We had like 6 movie stations. I never got to bed before 4:00 A.M.

Western Michigan University

I'd set my alarm so I'd have time to play a little 'Bond' before going to class—3 hours later I'd still be there—having totally missed class

Albion College

Instant Messaging is awful . . . it sucks up hours!

Junior, Journalism, UCLA

My roommate didn't know anybody on the entire floor, let alone in the dorm. He spent his whole first semester in chatrooms and game rooms.

Junior, English, University of Maryland

The first few weeks are great! You're meeting people, partying, no tests, no papers—then, **WHAM! You've got everything due in the same week!** If you weren't hitting the books right along, you'll spend the rest of the term digging yourself out!

Senior, Political Science, University of California, Santa Cruz

My brother, who's not in college, works 40 or 50 hours a week at his job. When I'm sick of studying I try to ask myself if I've put in that many hours. It's **definitely a reality check**. You need to think of school as your job.

Junior, Engineering, Notre Dame

"Where else is 15 hours a week considered a 'Full Load'?"

T-shirt worn by Michigan State University Student

RX: For good grades . . . PAARRTY!!!

College was *the* best time . . . I never missed a party *AND* I got great grades! The trick is to get up each morning and plan exactly what you want to do that night—party or whatever. Then tell yourself you can't go until you're done studying. It's like a reward. If I thought nothing was going on I'd waste the whole day and end up falling asleep in front of the TV at night.

Graduate, English, Ohio University

CLUE #2 Time Management!

I can't even say I'm on probation because of partying. I just became **a big couch potato.** For the first time in my life there wasn't anyone to tell me what to do or when to do it, so I didn't do anything—including study.

Freshman, Engineering, Michigan State University

TIME...

Study between classes. I spent a lot of time watching TV during the day until I figured out that if I *studied*, I could have my nights free. Don't go back to the dorm between classes. Find someplace to study. *John Carroll University*

Stay out of bed. *Any* time I didn't have classes, I slept. It's a *bad* habit to get into. *Rollins College*

Prioritize. I got so involved with club activities in my major that my grades were barely high enough to *get into* the major. *Michigan State University*

. . . Use it or lose it!

Make a calendar for the entire semester. I combine the dates from all the course syllabi onto *one* calendar and hang it where I can see it *daily*. It's a visual thing. You have to *see* it. *University of Wisconsin*

Set specific 'study hours.' For me, the toughest part of studying is getting started. I set aside a specific time for every day. It's like going to a job; you *have* to be there. *Cornell University*

Make lists. In high school you can do it when it comes to mind or when someone reminds you. In college there's too much to remember and *nobody's* going to remind you! *Adelphi University*

"A daily planner keeps you honest . . .

. . . I haven't exactly been the poster child for planning, especially as a freshman and sophomore, but it's become my 'main thing.' College assignments are mostly reading so there's no homework to hand in. The 'I don't have any homework tonight' feeling can snowball instantly into hundreds of unread pages or a project you're just starting the night before it's due. My planner keeps me in touch with reality."

Senior, Government, Franklin and Marshall College

Stress-busters!

Break assignments down! If you have a 400-page book to read . . . assign yourself so many pages per week. The end of the semester is *always* crunch time . . . don't make it worse!

Junior, Economics, SUNY/Stony Brook

Gather all the syllabi during the first week of classes and write down the due date for every single paper, project, test or whatever. You'll see instantly which weeks are potential killers.

Junior, English, Wake Forest

" **If you do nothing else in college, at least *go to class!***

Junior, Business, Miami University

"

Just *Go!*

"80% of success is just showing up"
—Woody Allen

Even if I'd partied all night, I dragged my body to class. Other people's notes don't work . . . *you have to hear it yourself.*

Graduate, English, Indiana University

Sitting in a classroom is the easiest part of college and it cuts study time in half. Why make it hard on yourself—*go!*

Senior, Journalism, University of Iowa

Instructors take it personally if you cut a lot. Not having an attendance *requirement* doesn't mean they won't take it out on your grade.

Junior, Education, Central Michigan University

I used to think the first couple of classes were a waste because everyone's still dropping and adding. **Wrong!** That's when the instructor announces changes in the syllabus and when you should decide whether to drop the class.

Junior, Business, University of Alabama

Talk about horror stories . . . I had one of those classes where you decide you'll learn more by reading the book than by going to class. I cut quite a few, including the one when a change in the final exam date was announced.

Senior, Communications, University of Toledo

"It's not how smart you are—everyone is.
It's whether you know how to study.
I see really bright guys that get "nothing"
grades and average guys that get 4-points.

Senior, Economics, University of Florida

Grinding It Out

"Of course it's hard! It's supposed to be hard!
If it wasn't hard everyone would do it!"
–Tom Hanks, A League of Their Own

Teachers are in your face every day in high school, so it's easy to stay on track and keep up the pace. It doesn't work that way in college. You set your own pace. If you don't study, it's your problem . . ..

Sophmore, Advertising, University of Florida

My roommate *never* studied and got great grades. It took me a while to face the fact that *I* couldn't do that. While he kicked back and had a good old time, I dragged myself to the library. It was frustrating, but that's life. You have to do what works best *for you*.

Senior, Communications, University of Toledo

Don't Get
BEHIND!!!

The biggest difference between high school
and college is the *amount of reading*. It's
impossible to catch up it you get behind.

Sophomore, Biology, Kalamazoo College

Ouch ... only 36% of entering freshman studied 6 hours or more per week in high school.*

> I'm studying 25% less these last two years than I did my first
> two and my GPA is a full point higher. It took learning how and
> *what* to study.
>
> *Senior, Government, Franklin and Marshall College*

Whether you're in a lecture or reading an assignment, always keep
asking yourself the same question . . .

"Will this be on the exam?"

Senior, Music, Murray State University

Read your class notes *FIRST* when studying for a test . . . *THEN* go over the readings. Your eyes will skim right past the crap and focus on what's important. If it wasn't mentioned in class, it probably won't be on the test.

Senior, Government, Franklin and Marshall

Avoid mindless reading by outlining. It forces you to zero in on concepts and organize your thoughts . . . then that's what you study before a test.

Senior, Architecture, New Jersey Institute of Technology

Get your butt to discussion groups even if they're not mandatory. It's easier to learn the material and it forces you to formulate your own ideas, which is very helpful for essay exams.

Senior, Education, University of Massachusetts

Where to do it . . . (study!)

Get out of the room! You'll end up talking on the phone, watching TV, cleaning out drawers—just about anything to avoid studying!

Graduate, Economics, Rollins College

Studying in bed is an illusion. After 15 minutes, you're zonked.

Junior, Anthropology, Macalester College

I know too many people at the library . . . **I study for tests at Krogers.** It's perfect . . . quiet, soft music, and when I need a break I cruise the aisles and pick up samples.

Senior, Marketing, Ohio University

Timing is everything . . .

Figure out when you're most efficient. **I was brain dead by 10 or 11 o'clock at night**—but that's when I started studying because *that's when everyone studies*. I'd have to read some things *10 times* for it to sink in! Finally, I realized that studying during the day was a lot better for *me*—and faster. There are so many cool, fun things to do in college . . . you don't want to be studying all the time.

Senior, Engineering, MIT

"I write better at night, read better in the morning and my classes go better in the afternoon."

Study Groups . . .

My study group saved me! I could take the time to talk through something and people in the group would pick up on what I was missing. With 30–40 kids in a classroom, professors can't do that.

Graduate, Engineering, Milwaukee School of Engineering

I don't believe in study groups. The logistics are difficult and they waste time. The buddy system works much better. A friend and I have almost every class together. Before tests or writing papers, we bounce things off one another . . . between the two of us, there isn't much we've missed.

Senior, Marketing, Ohio University

"I'd sit in class and stare out the window at the squirrels. They've got a cool nest in the tree.

Senior, Engineering, MIT

Group Projects

They're a pain! BUT, I've learned so much from brainstorming ideas and solving problems with other people.

Sophomore, Engineering, Drexel University

We left one guy to do the 'wrap-up' and turn it in . . . Guess who was a 'no show' the day the project was due? ALWAYS make sure everyone has a copy of the completed project prior to the due date.

Senior, Engineering, University of Michigan

There's always someone who likes to impress everyone with how much he knows. Include him in your group.

Senior, Business, University of Toledo

Classroom Cues

Little tips for big classes

Sit front and center. I can tell you what every person in class is wearing and not much of anything else when I sit in the back. It's like private tutoring . . . you get all your questions answered.

Sophomore, Art, Bowling Green University

It was *incredible* how much easier Chemistry was when I began reading the assignments *BEFORE* the lecture. It was like a different course.

Sophomore, Engineering, University of Michigan

***Always* get the phone number** of at least one person in every class in case you can't read your notes or remember the assignment.

Senior, Education, University of Tennessee

Big tips for little classes

Don't be late or leave early. It really ticks profs off. Besides that's when they usually make announcements or get to the point. The entire hour may be summed up in the last 5 minutes.

Sophomore, English, DePaul University

Volunteer to answer questions you *do* know so you won't be called on for the ones you don't.

Junior, Psychology, Colgate University

"You might as well 'let one rip' as have your cell phone go off in class . . . it's embarrassing."

"'Class participation' is a euphemism for 'make a good impression' . . .

. . . I have friends who hardly say a word in class but they do the other things that instructors appreciate—go to class, do the work, and hand it in on time."

Senior, Government, Franklin and Marshall

There were only sixty-three kids in my entire high school class—**_no way_ was I gonna raise my hand in a lecture with 300!** Eventually I started keeping a list of my questions and talking with the professor during his office hours . . . or I used e-mail.

Sophomore, Advertising, University of Florida

PROFPOINTERS

Classroom No-No's

Don't call me Mrs. . . . I'm 'Dr.' or 'Professor.' *Iowa State University*

Don't ask questions that show you haven't read the assignment. *DePaul University*

Make eye contact during lectures—at least, keep 'em open. *Indiana University*

Don't ask, 'What can I do to bring up my grade?' if you haven't been to class. *Rutgers*

I hate excuses. Tell it like it is and I'm likely to give you a break. *Albion College*

Don't put down other student's thoughts or opinions. *Michigan State University*

Make the most of lousy profs . . .

I keep the syllabus or course outline in the front of my notebook so that I can figure out what the point of the lecture is. You can't always tell.

Junior, Psychology, Southern Illinois University

I hated his class. The lectures were deadly. I finally forced myself to drop by during office hours. Somehow, after discussing a few points and getting to know him, his lectures seemed more interesting. At least, I could stay awake.

Junior, Education, Central Michigan University

PROFPOINTERS
E-mail Ettiquette

I'm not going to do a lecture by e-mail . . . ask a classmate what you missed if you weren't in class. *Odessa College*

It's NOT Instant Messaging! Use correct punctuation, spelling and grammar. A proper salutation and closing wouldn't hurt either. *UCLA*

Delete all the unnecessary garbage upfront and don't forward chain mail. *Oberlin*

I hate aliases. Include your name, course and section. *University of Oklahoma*

Don't avoid face-to-face conversation by using e-mail. *University of Iowa*

DON'T USE ALL CAPS! *SUNY/Stony Brook*

e-shrewd?

From: Joe Blow <blowj@msu.edu>
To: Professor Smith <smithphd@msu.edu>
Date: Thursday, Dec 14, 2000, 1:06 PM

Hey, Mrs. Smith, this is Joe saying hello! I was concerned about my grade in class. I'm not too sure how many days I missed, but I was recently informed by one of my peers that I may have missed 7+ days.

I know that if this is accurate I may receieve a 0.0 in the class. If so, could you please take this into consideration: although most of those days that I missed class was of pur laziness, in total honestly, at least 3 of those days, including the last day, i was under the weather. By the way, as a result of missing a day a while ago, I was not too sure how to put up a webpage and therefore will not be posting my paper on my page since it's non existant. Anyway, I hope that your christmas goes well and have a good vacation.
Joe Blow

PS. If I can get some help anytime soon, I'll try to get my webpage up andfinished before friday.

e-screwed!

From: Professor Smith <smithphd@msu.edu>
To: Joe Blow <blowj@msu.edu>
Date: Thursday, Dec 14, 2000, 2:37 PM

Dear Joe,

Your peers are right and you have missed way over seven days of class. Additionally, you did not do all the assignments or participate in class, and your missing web page is the result of not coming to class or getting in touch with me. Also, I should point out that tomorrow is the last day of finals and this is the very first time you have contacted me about your attendance and performance.

Unfortunately, you will receive a 0.0 in the class.

Sincerely,
Professor Smith

This e-mail correspondence is verbatim. Names have been changed to protect the guilty.

"I'd think to myself "I don't need to write that down, I'll remember it." A few days later, it was like "*what* did he say . . .?"

Junior, Economics, Duke University

Note: Scientifically speaking, you lose 70% of information within 24 hours.

Notes on Notetaking

School's never been easy for me so tape recording my classes helped *a lot*. I still took notes, but I could *relax and listen better* to what was being said because I always knew that I could "fast forward" to anything I needed to hear again.

Graduate, Management, Ferris State University

Not everything a prof says is important. But if you haven't read the assignments *before* the lecture you'll end up writing down every word anyway because you don't know what is and what isn't.

Junior, Biology, University of Michigan

Note: Get the instructor's permission to record the lecture.

Listen . . . Think . . . SUMMARIZE!!!

I had tons of notes—I copied *every word* the professor said. Actually, I was so busy writing that **I didn't *understand* a thing . . ..**

Junior, Criminal Justice, Saint Joseph's University

Watch the eyes. If the instructor looks down at his notes before speaking, the next sentence is probably important.

Senior, English, Rutgers University

Note-taking services are the best thing going. Use them to fill in the gaps—*not* in place of going to class!

Junior, Geology, Arizona State University

Pay attention to when you're not paying attention. It's impossible to keep your mind from wandering. Know when you're doing it and mark the spot in your notes so you can get the information later.

Junior, Business, Marquette University

Listen for . . .

KEY PHRASES

"to sum it up . . ."

"remember that . . ."

"in other words . . ."

"in my opinion . . ."

"the turning point . . ."

"notice that . . ."

"point #1, #2, etc."

"the basic reason . . ."

"a prime example . . ."

"in conclusion . . ."

I lost a notebook with *six weeks* of notes in it! Your name, phone, course, and section number should be on *every* book you own.

Junior, Political Science, Ohio State University

Instead of doing nothing between classes, I clean up my notes. If I don't re-read and clarify them sometime the same day, they never make sense later.

Junior, Labor Studies, Saint Joseph's University

"I use a yellow highlighter for what's important and hot pink for what's *really* important."

Tricks of the trade . . .

Be creative. I use a four-color pen, draw pictures, whatever it takes to make notes memorable.

Speak up. Don't be afraid to ask an instructor to slow down if he's going too fast.

Date your notes. It's easier to refer to your notes or compare them with others if they're dated.

One's good. Two's better. If I miss a class, I get notes from two different people. It's easier to pinpoint which information is really important.

> **In high school there were *zillions* of tests, quizzes, reports, extra credit . . . you name it. In college, it might be just a midterm and a final. If you mess up on one, your grade's shot!**

Senior, Education, University of Tennessee

Test Tips

1 Talk with the instructor before tests.

The odds are against you on first tests because you have no idea what to expect. I make a point of seeing the prof a few days before, just to make sure I'm "focusing on the right material." In other words, I want HOT TIPS. Taking a couple of "confused" classmates along makes him even more cooperative. Don't waste your time with TA's unless they know what's on the test. Some do, some don't.

Senior, Marketing, Ohio University

"Make-up tests are 100% harder."

Find old exams.

Hustling old tests is worth the effort. Profs seldom change them much. Even if they do, an old test will tell you which concepts you're expected to know and how well to know them. Check with students who have taken the course, the department, fraternity test files, the library, or the professor himself.

Senior, Management Information Systems, Ohio University

You gotta *UNDERSTAND.*

High school is memorization and regurgitation. Here you have to think. I remember bombing the first test after studying my brains out. Some of that stuff I swore I'd never seen before. It's called "applying the principle." You have to *understand the concept* well enough to see how it relates to something you've never discussed in class. That's where most kids get killed.

Junior, Engineering, Notre Dame

"Caffeine pills will give you the attention span of a flea."

4 Know the vocabulary of the course.

T.A.s are looking for key words and phrases, and not much else when there's 200 to 300 essay tests to correct. The more you use, the better your grade. Actually, if you don't understand the terminology well, you'll have trouble with multiple choice and true/false tests too.

Graduate, Marketing, University of Wisconsin

Lack of sleep prevents memory consolidation and problem-solving.

Make the most of quizzes.

Quizzes are an easy way to boost your grade because they
cover fewer chapters. It's your chance to make up for what you're
going to screw up on the final.

Senior, Marketing, Ohio University

Scantrons error.

Computerized test-scoring isn't perfect. Smudges can kill you. If
your grade seems incorrect, ask to see the answer sheet. It meant a
full grade for me . . ..

Graduate, Physiology, Michigan State University

7 Learn from your mistakes.

Some profs only post the test scores and never return the actual test. It's a pain, but ask to review the corrected test in his office so you know exactly what you missed. Otherwise, you'll repeat the same mistakes the next time.

Sophomore, No Preference, Michigan State University

The average SAT score of 1300 millionaires surveyed was 1190 (AP, 2000).

**Grades stress you out . . .
learning draws you in.**

Junior, English, University of Maryland

The ABC's of GPA's

Grade grubbing . . .

Grade errors happen, but most kids just figure they didn't do well on the exam and don't bother to check, especially if it's during the summer. The 2.0 I got in a class was supposed to have been a 2.5—not a big difference, but enough to get me off probation.

Junior, Communications, Michigan State University

Always **go over a test after it's graded** to make sure there aren't any errors and to see if you can "milk" it for a few more points. Just don't overdo it. Profs get ticked.

Senior, Psychology, Adelphi University

Ask the T.A. to reread a paper if you think it deserves a better grade. I've never *not* been given the extra points.

Senior, H.R.I., Michigan State University

Ask for extra credit or to rewrite a test or paper you've bombed. Some profs won't let you, but most will.

Senior, Accounting, Indiana University

Don't question an instructor's grading in front of other students. He'll be reluctant to help you.

Senior, English, Denison University

When "easy" doesn't do it . . .

Tough courses psyche me up. I'm more disciplined because I know I have to be, so my grades are better.

Senior, Accounting, Valparaiso University

The trouble with **"gut" courses** is that instead of using them as an opportunity to grab a good grade, you just blow them off and end up getting a C . . . or worse. They really ARE easy if you GO to class and DO the work.

Sophomore, Economics, Williams College

Things that 'Don't Count' (that really do)

Attendance. Profs will hammer you on the details of anything you write or say if you haven't been coming to class even when there's no attendance requirement. An answer that is viewed as 'a good effort' if you're in class regularly is likely to be considered BS if you haven't.

Senior, Government, Franklin and Marshall College

Homework. Homework may only be 10% of your grade but it really impacts way more than that. It's not only your opportunity to learn, but if turned in regularly, it tells the instructor you're really trying. If you're anywhere close, you'll get the higher grade.

Graduate, Biology, MIT

DROP It!!!

It's not a sin to drop a class. If you're in over your head, **don't take the hit** of a poor grade. It's discouraging and can ruin a GPA.

Sophomore, Premed, Cornell University

Note: Make sure you know the final date for dropping a class, with and without a refund, and whether it will affect your financial aid.

Help, I've fallen . . .

REPEAT RULES

Repeat an "F" as soon as possible. It's the quickest way to raise a GPA.

Don't bother repeating a 1.0 or a 1.5 unless you know you can do considerably better than a 2.0—or a higher grade is *required*.

DO repeat a low grade if the course is a "building block" for a series of courses you'll need . . . *especially MATH!*

Repeat courses at a junior college. The transfer repeat usually wipes out the original grade—at a cheaper price.

Note: Repeat rules vary among colleges. Check with your adviser.

> **An average student can get the same results as a smart one if he plays his cards right.**
>
> Senior, English, Denison University

Gaining the Edge

It's weird, you're the one who's only eighteen years old, but it's up to you to make the effort to talk with Ph.D.s if you want them to get to know you. I always try to find out what they're into, what research they're doing. If it's monkeys . . . I ask about monkeys.

Junior, Michigan State University

I got an A+ in one class and a D+ in another on *the exact same paper!* The A+ was from a T.A. I'd talked with a lot, and the D+ from one I hadn't.

Junior, Environmental Science, University of Michigan

Don't underestimate the power of kissing butt!

Junior, Sociology, University of Colorado

THINK
THINK
THINK About It . . .

Your grade on everything you write . . . tests, term papers, whatever . . . gets down to one opinion—the instructor's. If he likes you and thinks you're putting in effort, it can be **the difference between an A and a C.**

Junior, Business, Miami University

Attitude is everything . . .

Instructors will bend over backwards to help kids who are really trying. Make every effort to let them know you are.

Junior, Journalism, University of Iowa

If you go in thinking "this sucks, the prof's a dork," you'll hate the course. Just sit there and figure you're gonna make the most of it. I aced a really nasty course that way. I stopped by the prof's office once a week just to talk. He loved me. Too bad I didn't figure that out in high school.

Sophomore, Lansing Community College

Write thank-you notes to guest speakers and file their names in your Rolodex. You never know when one of them might be able to help you with a summer job or internship.

Senior, English, Aquinas College

MENTOR magic . . .

A friend of mine worked on a project with one of our professors. That relationship eventually allowed him to accompany the prof to Poland and to present research to several economic groups. He was later **recommended for Phi Beta Kappa** by the professor and ultimately accepted at a prestigious law school. I could have been the one volunteering for that project . . ..

Senior, Economics, Hope College

It's who you know . . .

I wasn't exactly the best student, by a long shot, but I had established a good relationship with an instructor in my major, and he recommended me for the internship. Voila! Six months in the Virgin Islands!

Senior, Hospitality Management, Michigan State University

. . . and who you don't.

Grad school applications ask for three *personal* recommendations from undergraduate faculty. I barely remembered any of their *names!* I know they didn't remember mine!!!

Graduate, Telecommunications, Michigan State University

> ## *"Find one person who really cares about you surviving . . ."*

Senior, English, College of St. Benedict and St. John's University

What separated me from the masses was 'connecting' with a faculty member. I didn't even know what the possibilities were until he laid out a 'roadmap' and showed me a few shortcuts to get there. He made learning about the field exciting and was always there to listen and offer constructive criticism. When my confidence was shaky, he reminded me that I could do it.

Graduate, Neuro-Biology, University of Michigan

Make-A-Mentor

Independent Study. A one-on-one course with a professor of your choice. Just ask whomever you'd like to work with—*or get a recommendation from.*

Student/Research Assistant. Is there a professor who you enjoy or teaches a course you're interested in? Ask to be a student assistant. OR, ask to work on a prof's research project. He'll love you for it . . . *and help you.*

Campus Jobs/Activities. These allow administrators and faculty to get to know you. You'll have frequent, informal access to great advice.

Seminar Courses. Very small courses allow you to establish rapport with instructors so you can easily tap their wisdom and resources.

Advisors. There are good ones who will become great mentors IF you see them often and during non-busy periods.

My biggest regret when I look back at college is not having used the office hours.

Graduate, Physiology, Michigan State University

"Knowing your prof is huge! It's the one thing I do from day one."

Learn who the professors are. If one of them is an expert in a field you're interested in or he's from a grad school you're thinking about, then he's the one you want to get to know and his recommendation is the one you want to have.

Graduate, Biology, Columbia University

You can cut study time in half just by chatting with instructors during office hours. They'll pinpoint what is and what isn't important in the lectures and readings. Most are glad to talk with you since they have to be there anyway.

Senior, Education, University of Tennessee

***Before* asking** a prof for help, read the assignments. It's obvious if you haven't, and she'll resent you wasting her time.

Senior, Political Science, Western Michigan University

PROFPOINTERS

Who impresses 'em . . .

I'm impressed with students who make a point to introduce themselves and tell me their goals. Chances are I can help them get there or I know someone who can. *University of Connecticut*

I like to see students who have an interest outside of themselves and their grades. They have something that *I* can learn from *them*. *Michigan State University*

The students who really impress me may not be the "best" students . . . they're the ones who are really interested. Their focus isn't on grades as much as on really learning. *Iowa State University*

Some students seem to stay connected even after a class has ended—they e-mail, stop by . . . whatever. I enjoy following their progress, giving them advice, writing recommendations. *Miami University, Ohio*

PROFPOINTERS **. . . and who doesn't**

It's a dead giveaway when students ask questions designed to find out how little they can get by with. "How many pages do I *have* to read?" tells me that you're not very interested in a subject that is *my life's work*. Michigan State University

I'm not gonna go the extra mile for students who give me even the slightest signal that they're not interested in my subject. If you're not, you'd better fake it. Texas A & M

Students who don't go to class are a total turnoff. I write 'em off. Bowling Green State University

It's interesting that my full-time college students always give excuses for late papers and missing classes while my part-time students who are working and raising families seldom do. University of Tampa

" It's tough to have to lay out a "plan"
when you don't know where you're going. "

Senior, Economics, University of Connecticut

The MAJOR Dilemma

Don't just sit there . . .

I probably spent more time checking out used cars than checking out majors. I worried about it a lot but I never got off my butt and did anything to find out what each major was really about. When the time came that I had to decide, I didn't have much more information than I did as a freshman—it was kind of like throwing a dart.

Senior, Economics, University of Connecticut

As a senior I was still scrambling—I didn't know what in the world was even out there. I ended up taking a Career Decision-Making course and could kick myself for not having done it as a freshman or sophomore. I not only learned about careers but about me.

Senior, Psychology, Michigan State University

F R O M   T H E   A D V I S O R

F R O M   T H E   A D V I S O R

ADVISOR

Strategies for Making a Choice

Talk to professors in courses you enjoy about what majors and careers are related to that field.

Know what's available. In addition to the majors, get a list of minors, cognates, specializations, or whatever. They add focus to a degree and make you more marketable.

Go to Career Fairs and Grad School presentations. You'll get an idea of what's out there and how to position yourself for it.

Use the career center. Counselors, testing, and career files are all there to help you.

Talk to people in the career you think you'd like about what's going on in that field and how to get there. Ask to job shadow.

Due to a lot of screw-ups my freshman year, my major isn't exactly what I'd like it to be. Unfortunately, by the time I decided what that was, I'd already taken—and bombed—some of the required courses. It's like if you're even thinking about a major, find out the requirements!

Senior, Economics, University of Florida

Biology was always my thing so that's what I majored in. At the time, I didn't realize there were lots of other majors related to that field that could have opened up totally different career options. . .

Senior, Biology, Michigan State University

"I love __fill in the blank__ but I don't know how I'd make a career of it."
(Sports, music, cars, nature, computers—whatever your interests.)

IMAGINE

How could I be paid to:

Write about it?

Perform it?

Create a product
related to it?

Provide a service to
people interested in it?

Talk about it?

Assist people who do
it?

Sell a product related
to it?

Learn about it?

*Note: Adapted from Patrick Combs' Major in Success (Ten Speed Press, 1994),
a terrific book for helping students connect interests, majors, and careers.*

Do *your* thing . . .

. . . not your parents'. If your parents want you to be a biologist and you're an artist, you'll never stay awake studying. It's too hard to get decent grades if you don't like your major.

Junior, Sociology, University of Colorado

The money motive. Don't make choosing your major a "career move." Pick what you really enjoy. Chances are the money will follow. If it doesn't, at least you'll like your job.

Graduate, Economics, Carleton College

The tunnel-vision trap. I just picked a major and stuck to the requirements so I'd be sure to graduate in four years. I keep thinking there were other majors I'd have enjoyed more . . ..

Senior, Political Science, University of California, Santa Cruz

Get real . . .

Until the day he flunked out, my roommate insisted that he was an "engineering major"—completely ignoring the fact that he was pretty bad in math and science. If he'd been realistic about his major, he'd still be here.

Senior, Accounting, Indiana University

Go with your natural ability. It probably isn't in a major where you have to kill yourself to get good grades.

Graduate, Marketing, University of Wisconsin

EXPERIENCE Counts . . .

Internships are where it's at. Mine helped me figure out that I hated accounting, and it also helped me get my first job. It's a good way to test the waters *and* build a résumé.

Graduate, Business, Albion College

I'd have given up on an engineering degree because of all the math if I hadn't had a summer job with an engineering firm. It made me realize that's the career I really want. Now I'm willing to do what it takes to get there—and that's math.

Sophomore, Engineering, Michigan State University

Forget Burger King . . . find a summer job or volunteer doing something related to a career you may be interested in. It'll help you decide whether you are.

Junior, Business, Marquette University

I'd be heading to grad school *in the wrong field* if it weren't for one thing—*volunteering!* I had no experience in anything other than retail sales until this fall when I started volunteering at a local agency. Everyone says, 'find your passion.' I think I have . . . *just in the nick of time*.

Senior, Psychology, Michigan State University

I always wanted to be a nurse—*I thought.*
It wasn't until I started working in a hospital,
AFTER struggling through a year and a half of tough
science courses, that I realized **I don't even like
being around sick people!** A little volunteer work
or summer job would have told me that a lot sooner.

Junior, Education, University of Michigan

For love . . .

My parents were so worried when I told them I wanted to major in animal science. They were afraid that since I had decided against vet school I would end up doing kennel clean-up at $8 an hour. I loved animals and stuck with my plan . . . trust me, *it's worked!*

Graduate, Animal Science, Ohio State University

. . . or $$$

I followed the money. Was I right? Well, no. But I wasn't really wrong either. I'm not in love with my job every single day, but it gives me freedom and yes, the money, to do what I love outside of the office. It's a tricky choice. Money can't buy happiness but I think people can find a happy medium.

Graduate, Finance and Business Economics, Notre Dame

My advice is *DON'T* wait until your senior year to find out what the job prospects are in your major. If it's highly competitive, there are things you *need* to do along the way to make yourself more marketable—pick up a minor, learn a language, volunteer . . . whatever.

Senior, Economics, University of Connecticut

Find out which majors at your school are considered "tops" in their field. You *might* run across one you'd really like . . . and graduates from those majors are usually heavily recruited.

Graduate, Packaging, Michigan State University

"Major in something you enjoy as an undergraduate and make it marketable in grad school."

THE BIG PICTURE

You can be totally immobilized if you think of choosing a major as what you're going to do with **"the rest of your life!?!"** For most people, it isn't. Looking back, I think it makes sense to choose a major based on what you enjoy. You're more likely to be enthusiastic and that's what opens doors. Besides, most entry-level jobs require skills you'll learn in ANY major.

Graduate, Business, University of Tennessee

"Extraordinary drive comes from doing what you enjoy."
-Patrick Combs

Bottom Line: A JOB

Unless you're in engineering or accounting, or something specific like that, majors are pretty much interchangeable when it comes to getting a job. Eight of us were recently hired in this company, all with different majors.

Graduate, English, Indiana University

College grads will hold 4–5 jobs by the age of 34. (*US Dept. of Labor*)

I don't even know what kind of job to look for, let alone where to find it. I wish I'd majored in something that directed me to a specific career—teaching, dietetics, accounting, something like that.

Senior, Humanities, Michigan State University

. . . one year later.

I landed a great job that has absolutely nothing to do with my major. I got it because of my work experience, campus activities, and good recommendations from both.

Graduate, Humanities, Michigan State University

"When you first start college, you don't even know what questions to ask because you don't know what you should know . . ..

Senior, Education, St. Mary's College

Surviving 'The System'

Who has the answers . . .?

Be kind to secretaries. They can make your life a lot easier and usually know more about the rules and regulations than instructors.

Senior, Film, San Francisco City College

There are advisers and there are *advisers.* The best thing I did was find one who was willing to do more than just okay my schedule.

Senior, Economics, University of Florida

I always started with the R.A. If she couldn't answer a question, she knew who could.

Senior, Economics, Carleton College

***Everything's* in the catalog** and that's the problem. Use the index.

Junior, Microbiology, Michigan State University

F R O M   T H E   A D V I S O R

F R O M   T H E   A D V I S O R

ADVISOR

That's a Good Question . . . Ask It!

What's the last day to add or drop a class—with and without the 100% refund? Is a drop noted on the transcript?

What are the minimum number of credits allowed to maintain eligibility for financial aid, scholarships, academic honors, health insurance, or living in the dorm?

What are the deadlines for application to various majors?

Is a "repeat" averaged with the original grade or does it replace it? How many repeats are allowed?

Can courses be taken for credit only, no grade, otherwise known as pass/fail? Will all majors accept them?

Get It In Writing!!!

Universities are notorious for screwing up. Keep all your receipts, copies of drops, adds, *anything that you had to get official permission to do.*

Senior, English, Rutgers University

Someone I saw my freshman year told me—or I thought she did—that I could substitute one of my requirements with another course. By my senior year, whoever it was, was gone and **there was nothing noted in my file.** I had to take the course.

Senior, Marketing, Ohio University

If you're sick, don't just lie around your room until you're better. Notify the instructor and see a doctor at the health center to get medicine *AND* verification. Profs are leery of scams.

Senior, Business, University of Toledo

Pre-register!!! Grab what classes you can even if you're unsure. You can drop and add later.

Junior, Geology, Arizona State University

The Pass/Fail option is a good way to take courses you're weak in without destroying your GPA. BUT make sure which majors will or won't accept the credits.

Junior, Biology, University of Michigan

Transfer tips, tricks . . .

Don't hesitate to transfer if you can't get into the program you want. I knew I wanted to be a teacher, so when I wasn't accepted, I transferred. In the long run, no one cares *where* your degree's from.
Eastern Michigan University

Be prepared to hit the ground running when you transfer as a junior. You'll only have four semesters to establish your GPA. and it will be based on all upper level courses.
University of Colorado

Keep in touch with advisers at the school you want to transfer to. They'll tell you exactly which courses you should be taking and they'll know you're serious about transferring.
El Camino Junior College

I felt like a "freshman" with junior status when I transferred . . . I was lost. Believe me, you're pretty much on your own—there's no big orientation. Get involved in activities and make a point of connecting with faculty as soon as possible.
Michigan State University

. . . and traps.

Credits transfer, grades don't—which makes junior colleges a good place to take tough courses without destroying a GPA. Classes are smaller too, so you're likely to get more attention.

University of Florida

Beware of "equivalents." No way did the course I took at another college during the summer prepare me for the follow-up course at my own school. It's better to take the *last* course in a sequence at another college, *not the first*.

University of Michigan

When you're "explaining" a course you've taken somewhere else to the person deciding whether to accept that credit, make sure you *know the description of the "equivalent" course* at that school. A few well-chosen words or phrases can make all the difference.

Ohio University

Do it *before* you're a junior if you plan to take a course at a community college. Credits from a two-year school may not be accepted after that.

Michigan State University

Note: Transfer rules vary from college to college. Check yours.

F R O M   T H E   A D V I S O R

ADVISOR

Places to Go . . . People to See

Learning Center. Develop strategies for better test-taking, studying, note-taking, reading, etc.

Service-Learning. You'll find opportunities for volunteering in community agencies, schools, business, government, etc.

Student Services. Get information on research opportunities, mentor programs, student organizations, and overseas studies.

Career Counseling. Assessment tests and counselors will help you clarify goals and examine appropriate careers/majors.

Job Placement. Access to employers on and off campus, summer jobs and internships.

Note: Not every college refers to these services by the same name.

It's amazing how many things on this campus would really have been helpful if I'd known about them as a freshman instead of as a senior. **Nobody lays it out for you** . . . you have to find things yourself.

Senior, Accounting, University of Michigan

GOODAdvice

If I'd talked to an adviser instead of just my friends **I could have saved about $5,000** and a lot of grief. Between the classes I took that I didn't need and the semester I added by missing the application date to my major, a few visits to the advising office would have really paid off.

Senior, Nursing, Michigan State University

Don't believe everything you read. The printed requirements for majors aren't always up to date, or they'll accept a course that's not listed. I took a class I hated only to find that the requirement had been dropped.

Graduate, Michigan State University

You can mess up your graduation date if you miss a course that isn't offered every semester, especially if it's a prerequisite for other courses you need! Have an adviser review your four-year plan.

Junior, Chemical Engineering, M.I.T.

Want *GOOD* advice? Don't wait until the last minute to see advisers or professors. That's what everyone does . . . so they're too busy to help you beyond the bare minimum. On a slow day they'll give you all kinds of help.

Senior, Political Science, Western Michigan University

> **Everyone we interview has a 3.0.**
> **So what makes _you_ different?**

Job Recruiter

Smart Moves

Head's Up . . . Networking!

You can tell who's going to go places—they not only have good technical skills but they network like crazy.

Senior, Electrical Engineering, MIT

I'm glad I checked around . . . I found that the doctor at one of two animal clinics I was considering for a summer job was not only on the admissions committee at the Vet School but was well known in the field. That's the clinic I chose! The doctor took me to trade shows and seminars where I got to meet anyone and everyone in the industry. I also discovered that I preferred the business end of veterinary medicine.

Graduate, Animal Science, Ohio State University

Join a professional association related to your major. That's how I know what's going on in my field . . . their newsletter and online discussion group. If I need good stuff for a paper or want to know who to contact for a job, it's easy.

Junior, Horticulture, Michigan State University

I have the 'in' on everything that goes on in theatre—my *passion*— because I work as the assistant to the college's producer. I'll *always* have amazing people to go to for advice because of it.

Senior, Architecture/Theatre, New Jersey Institute of Technology

As a Student Assistant, the professor treated me more like a colleague than a kid. I got all the 'inside info' and by teaching others, I learned the topic so well I could do it in my sleep.

Senior, Art, Alfred University

Note: Student Assistant positions are available through the department or by contacting a professor directly.

JOIN!

Definitely join a club affiliated with your major. That's where you'll meet faculty and make contacts with people in your field. Guest speakers are just a year or two out of college so they're easy to talk to and usually willing to forward resumés to higher ups.

Senior, Accounting, Indiana University

As an undergrad I joined a lot of **'low commitment-high resumé groups.'** The reality is that when it comes to paring your resumé down to one page, that stuff goes. If you've done *zip* in the group—there's nothing you're proud of—then it's a waste of time.

Graduate, Communications, Weber State University

Do-It-Yourself!

It started with four of us who wanted to learn how to make the next great computer game . . . and now there are about 40 of us and weekly meetings! It's fun and a lot easier to have the resources and motivation of a group. I want to work in the computer game industry when I graduate but my concern has always been how to get IN! Companies probably get hundreds of e mails and resumés a day asking for jobs. *BUT*, how many will send a CD full of demo programs they have created and a story about the game programming group they helped found at a major university?!?

Junior, Engineering, Michigan State University

"I thought all the activities and clubs on campus were stupid because they didn't really do anything. Now that I'm in a career, I realize THAT was what THIS is all about!"

There's no downside to research projects. You often get paid, the hours are flexible, it looks good on a resumé and letters of recommendation tend to be stellar! Start looking around for one your freshman year.

Graduate, Animal Science, Ohio State University

Because I was pledging a fraternity my freshman year, I decided not to take part in the research program I'd been invited to join—thinking I'd do it later. Well, I never got around to it. When I see how 'well-connected' and focused people are that are in it, I realize **I really screwed up.**

Senior, Biology, University of Michigan

Nothing compares to the advice and encouragement you'll get and the connections you'll make when working with a faculty member on a research project.

Graduate, Psychology, University of Texas

"Professors know better than anyone who's doing what research. Ask."

Think Resumé

I had 3 different internships starting my freshman year. The variety really helped me define my career direction. *AND* because I'd had so much experience, I totally skipped the entry level position in my first job.

Graduate, Advertising, Western Michigan University

I always prefer job candidates who have had any kind of work experience, even if it's folding shirts at The Gap, to an applicant with only a formal education. If they've had an internship related to the field it's icing on the cake because **I know they understand what they're getting into.**

Vice-President of Human Resources

Hey, there's no Santa either . . .

Everyone talks about *'getting an internship'* . . . I
thought there must be some **'internship fairy'** that
just appears and hands 'em out. NOT! There may be
some available through your major or at the career
center but basically, you're on your own.

Junior, Sociology, University of Colorado

INTERNSHIPS . . .

Cold Calls. I just picked up the phone and asked for an appointment with Human Resources at a company I thought would be interesting to work at. I told them I'd work for free—which I would've—but they're paying me.

Michigan State University

Upperclassmen. Keep tabs on where upperclassmen and grads you know are working or interning. Ask them to pass on your resumé.

MIT

Career Fairs. Freshmen should definitely go just to check out what the possibilities are and who to contact. At least you know what you're gunning for.

Penn State University

Internet. A friend of mine found an internship with the Olympic Bobsled Team on the Internet. How cool is that?! *(Try internshipprograms.com, monster.com, interncenter.com)*

University of West Florida

64% of interns are eventually offered a job by their host employer.

. . . where to find them!

Faculty. I told my professor that I wanted to spend the summer in California and he gave me the names of colleagues I could contact for a job. Profs know people all over the country.

MIT

Volunteer. I set up my own internship with the Volunteer Coordinator at a local hospital. A friend of mine couldn't find a journalism internship so he offered to work on their newsletter.

Michigan Technological University

Contact 'associations.' Every career field has an association. Contact it for a list of intern positions—or ask if you could put your inquiry in their newsletter or listserv*.

Creighton University

Friends and family. It's always who you know . . . *or who your parents know*. But with friends of your family, you *really* don't want to screw up!

UCLA

*A listserv is an online discussion group related to a specific topic.

Never too late . . .

My smartest move . . . taking a 5th year! I could have graduated in four but by my senior year I was just getting on track. I'd just become a cheerleader which meant I got to carry a lot of good-looking women on my shoulders and I was working on a great research paper with a faculty member. I'm convinced that the extra time I had to do those things is what made my application to an Ivy League professional school stand out . . . yep, I got in!

Graduate, Neuro-Biology, University of Michigan

51.6% of freshmen graduate within 5 years. (*ACT, 1999*)

THE WEB VIRGIN'S GUIDE
TO CAMPUS COMPUTING

Password protect . . . so no one can use your computer without asking.

BACKUP! . . . to the hard drive *AND* a disk.

Don't store your disk with your laptop—they'll both get stolen.

Update your anti-virus software monthly—you do have it, *right?!*

Keep floppies and zip disks in a case, not loose in your bookbag.

Activate your 'auto save' feature.

Don't open unknown attachments—*especially '.exe' files.*

"All power strips are NOT surge protectors."

" I can still hear my dad's voice
after my first semester,
"What the hell are you doing with my money?" **"**

Junior, Economics, SUNY/Stony Brook

I visited the financial aid office during the summer before my freshman year. Classes hadn't started so they weren't swamped yet. It was **the best thing I ever did.** The adviser took a lot of time with me and got to know my situation. From then on, I always requested him. Over the course of my college career, he saw to it that I got some serious cash.

Graduate, Biology, University of Michigan

The best thing my parents did for me? Had their taxes done by February 2nd every year. There were no guessing games and no missing information on the financial aid form—so, *NO DELAYS IN MY AID!*

Graduate, Engineering, Milwaukee School of Engineering

*I celebrated not having to fill out FAFSA forms
more than getting my diploma.*

Graduate, Engineering, Milwaukee School of Engineering

Beg . . . or at least, plead your case. Computers only know numbers and those don't tell the whole story. My mom had lost her job and couldn't contribute anything, let alone the $20,000 the government had calculated. Once the aid office heard the *whooole* story, I not only got the aid, but a scholarship!

Sophomore, Computer Engineering, Michigan Technological University

"Borrow only what you *NEED!!!*"

I made $25,000 for ten hours of work! My mom pretty much had to put a gun to my head to get me to fill out scholarship applications. I ended up getting two out of the 6 or 7 I applied for . . . *nice hourly rate!*

Senior, Engineering, MIT

People don't think to apply for scholarships to their churches or parents' places of employment *(even if they don't work there anymore)*. And corporations are always generous. Here in Atlanta we have Delta, Coca-Cola . . . and *Ted*.*

Senior, Psychology, Spelman College

All they need to do is write a brief essay, list community involvement—and they get the money! **We have scholarships we can't give away** because kids won't write the essay.

Alumni Scholarship Fund Office

* CNN's Ted Turner

I'm so mad at myself for not applying for any of the
scholarships that were available. I didn't get one coming
out of high school so I never gave it a second thought in
college . . . **dumb!**

Senior, Human Communications, University of Connecticut

*Note: There are private grants and scholarships available to existing students,
often within the major. Check with your adviser.*

BANKING AND CHECKING . . .

"Debit cards are easy. You don't have to carry much cash or write as many checks—but you'd better know your balance."

"Choose a bank with a convenient ATM. If yours isn't, you'll end up using another and paying two bucks every time you need ten."

"Set up a checking account with a local bank asap. 'Starter checks' aren't accepted by most places so you'll be out of luck for like 30 days."

"No matter what, *DON'T* write your access code down on paper and send a friend to do your banking. *Borrow* money until you can do it yourself."

I love my debit card . . . I totally have no self control!
When the money's gone, it's gone. I just have to
make sure I know when that point is. After paying a few
$25 overdraft fees, I've learned.

Senior, Music Education, Murray State University

*Note: Get overdraft protection. It's worth it—as long as you don't use it as credit.
The interest can bury you.*

CREDIT CARDS . . .

"Don't use a credit card for anything you eat, wear, or listen to. Who wants to pay interest on a meal eaten a month ago?"

"Do the math . . . if you're only paying the minimum each month, the actual cost of the item is 3–4 times the original price."

"If you can't trust yourself to pay *on time, every month,* don't use a credit card. There's a $30 fee and your credit rating's trashed."

"Never get a cash advance on a credit card. The interest accumulates *daily* and will kill you."

"Use 'plastic' to pay tuition. The Frequent Flier points are *huge,* which means free air fare to and from school—or *maybe* Cancun?"

Credit cards are good to have in case of an emergency—*but* make sure you're clear on the definition of "emergency." For me it was every time I went into The GAP—**until my dad saw the bill.**

Sophomore, History, University of Pennsylvania

WHOA . . .

We do a credit check on all job applicants before hiring. It's based on retail accounts, gasoline cards, car loans—but primarily on **credit card history.**

Vice-President of Human Resources

THE PHONE BILL . . .

"Calling cards are the best deal! I got mine for 2.9 cents per minute—hard to beat that!"

"Don't call collect and especially don't bill to a third number. It's astronomical."

"My parents have an 800 number. I can call home whenever, wherever."

"Don't put the phone in your name if you can avoid it. It's a pain to divvy up the charges among roommates and a bigger pain to collect."

"Cell phones are great *IF* you get reception in your dorm! Sometimes I have to go outside to make a call—and Philadelphia isn't Florida!"

Sophomore, University of Pennyslvania

Cars on CAMPUS

Parking on campus is a nightmare. Out of *desperation* you always end up parking in restricted areas. I had to take out a short-term note just to pay off parking tickets and tow charges before I was allowed to register.

Senior, Telecommunications, Michigan State University

Note: Parents, you may be able to get lower auto insurance rates if your student is more than 100 miles from home and doesn't have a car at school.

A JOB !?!?!?

Don't get a job until after your freshman
year . . . or whenever you've figured out how
to manage your time.

Senior, Economics, University of Florida

77% of students expect to become millionaires. (*Wall Street Journal, 1999*)

It's a trade-off. I was working so many hours that I had to cut back on credits. In the long run, it's cost me. I'm taking longer to graduate and it'll be that much longer before I'm making *real* money.

Junior, Business, University of Alabama

If there's nothing much to do, I don't do much of anything, including study. I manage my time better when I'm working 15 to 20 hours a week.

Senior, Business, University of Toledo

Some kids just go to class . . . nothing else. A job gets you 'out there'—you meet more people and connect on different levels. It's important to work, even a few hours.

Senior, Biology, University of Michigan

A good piece of work . . .

Get a job in the office of your major. You'll get to know everyone from the secretaries to the dean, all of whom can be very helpful. If any great opportunities come along, you'll be the first to know.

Senior, Environmental Science, Indiana University

50% of full-time students work part-time. (NACE, 2000)

QUICK TIPS

"The good jobs go fast. Start looking early."

"Work your tail off in the summer so you don't have to work during the school year."

"Find a job in something related to your major."

"Don't work in restaurants unless you wait tables. That's where the money is."

"Find a job where you can study."

"Don't work more than 20 hours a week if you're carrying a full load; ten to fifteen is better."

"Kids bring all 500 CD's and they're left with 200 at the end of the first week. It leaves them scarred for the rest of college."

Senior, Accounting, Indiana University

Crime Stoppers

Label everything . . .

It's just like going to camp—put your name on everything! There's a guy walking around campus in what I *know* is *my* $200 jacket, but I've got no proof. I'm *ticked* every time I see him!

Senior, Marketing, Ohio University

I had my laptop engraved with my driver's license number and recorded the model, serial numbers, and receipts of anything valuable that I was taking to school.

Junior, Social Work, Rutgers University

Note: Your parent's homeowner's insurance may extend to your personal property while living in the dorm.

Keep your eyes on the prize . . .

Some people shop in the laundry more often than the mall. Don't leave clothes in the washer or dryer and expect them to be there when you return!

Senior, Accounting, University of Michigan

Gone . . . my Palm Pilot, Oakley sunglasses, two graphing calculators, and all my class notes—*two days before the exam.* So much for leaving your bookbag on the table while you're in the food line.

Sophomore, Michigan State University

Watch your computer access number. Someone can mess around with your schedule or drop your classes and you have no way to prove it wasn't you that did it.

Senior, Packaging, Michigan State University

Leave the good stuff at home . . .

Don't bring an expensive bike. Even with the best lock it'll get ripped off piecemeal . . . or rust.

Ohio State University

I don't know *what* ever happened to an expensive gold bracelet I brought. It just disappeared.

DePaul University

Don't prop doors. Even if *you* don't care about your worldly possessions, your roommate or suitemates will.

University of Rhode Island

Avoiding creeps, perverts, & lowlifes

Know the campus bus schedule and plan on leaving before the last run of the night. *Michigan State University*

Stick to public places when you go out with someone you don't know well. *University of Iowa*

Keep your finger on the button. Mace or pepper spray won't do any good in your purse. *Columbia University*

Know how you're getting home before you go! *Iowa State University*

Let people know where you're going and when you'll be back. If your plans change, call. *Butler University*

Don't use ATMs at night, especially if you're alone. *University of Pennsylvania*

"It's like there's this image of 'college' you need to live up to—wild parties, no sleep, cutting classes. It's easy to get sucked into, especially if you're not quite sure why you're here."

Junior, Geology, Arizona State University

Partying & Stuff

Everyone's a little 'needy' when they start college—you latch on to whomever. I spent every weekend drinking my brains out with the same people before I realized it was kinda boring.

Junior, Advertising, University of Florida

I wish someone had told me how useless and expensive drinking is. It's taken me 3 semesters to raise my GPA.

Junior, Economics, SUNY/Stony Brook

We buy 3 pitchers of beer and 3 pitchers of Coke. That's what college is about—making your own decisions. As long as you're around people who respect yours, it's okay.

Junior, Economics, Notre Dame

You can always tell freshmen. They act like they've just been let off the leash.

Senior, Business, Northern Illinois University

It's hard to believe what a straight-arrow I was in high school . . . National Honor Society and the whole thing. I've basically screwed myself so far in college. My entire freshman year "went up in smoke," if you know what I mean. I barely even remember the names of my courses, let alone going to them. **I guess the party's over**—along with my scholarship.

For the Record

Really, you don't *have* to drink. The only time people think you're weird is when you sit around doing nothing. Just *go* to the parties. No one notices *what* you do once you're there.

University of California/Santa Cruz

Baby-sitting friends who are habitually tanked gets real old, real fast.

University of Wyoming

In college it's easy to do your own thing. If you don't drink, it's not a big deal.

Macalester College

Some schools can be anal about the rules on alcohol in the dorms. Be sure you know the consequences. Around here you'll get busted big time.

University of Arizona

A 12 oz. beer = 1 shot of liquor = 1 glass of wine

"Everyone likes to talk about how trashed they were
but I think a lot of it's just talk."

Junior, Economics, Notre Dame

FACT & FICTION

Students were asked to estimate the number of drinks consumed by their peers. It was then compared to the actual number.

		Estimated	Actual
Amount Consumed:	Men	7 drinks	3 drinks
	Women	5 drinks	2 drinks
Frequency:		3 times per week	1 time per week

Study by Montana State University and National Core Institute

Women absorb alcohol into the bloodstream faster and metabolize it slower than men.*

*www.brad21.org

The Unwritten Rule

There's a responsibility . . . friends take care of friends. You can do some dumb things when you're partying. Go in a group.

Senior, Biology, MIT

"I never thought drugging would be an issue . . . until one of my friends got drugged. Always get your own drink!"

"DON'T BE SO STUPID THAT YOU ACCIDENTALLY DIE."

Way Beyond Stupid

- Drinking a fifth of vodka through a beer bong

- Drinking and walking home alone

- Mixing prescription drugs with alcohol

- Drinking and driving

- Letting someone drunk drive you

- Drinking 21 shots on your 21st birthday

Excerpted from Harlan Cohen's Campus Life Exposed (Peterson's, 2000)

*www.brad21.org

If breathing is irregular, slow (less than 8 breaths per minute or more than 10 seconds between breaths), GET HELP!*

It is what it is. Once you've done something you can't erase it . . . but you can make sure you don't make the same mistake twice.

Junior, Special Education, Kent State University

"Don't go near a bedroom if you're high."

Dating DILEMMAS

If a girl even hints at "no" or "stop," pay attention. My friend was accused of rape, and even though the charges were eventually dropped, it was devastating to his family and he was dropped from the fraternity he was pledging.

Senior, Accounting, University of Michigan

Note: The highest incidence of sexual assault is among freshmen and is most likely to occur during the first 3 months on campus.

Know when to fold 'em . . .

Sports gambling is huge in the dorms and easy to get hooked on since it makes watching games with a bunch of guys really exciting. A friend of mine had to sell his Jeep to cover his losses . . . and *that* was calling "lock lines" which are supposed to be *sure* things.

Junior, Criminal Justice, Saint Joseph's University

I was losing twenty bucks a night just playing cards on our floor! It's easy to get sucked into that stuff when there's a bunch of guys around and you don't feel like studying.

Graduate, Business, Albion College

"Don't take your ATM card to the casino."

College towns are exciting. You meet people from different backgrounds with different values. Know what yours are and stick to them.

Junior, Economics, Duke University

"Go ahead, pierce whatever . . . but tattoos after you're 25 are sooo embarrassing!"

"I wouldn't want to pay money to have friends . . . but fraternity guys *do* meet a lot of girls.

Senior, Economics, University of Florida

To be or not to be . . .
GREEK

Greek musings . . .

At some schools you're either Greek, an athlete, or you sit around doing nothing on weekends. *Miami of Ohio*

It's a good way to make a big school feel small. Classes at most universities are huge and you really don't get to know anyone. Sororities make it easier, less isolating. *University of Iowa*

I'd miss a lot if I were wrapped up in a sorority. I'd rather be involved in campus sports, clubs, plays, and things like that. *M.I.T.*

Fraternities make it easy to socialize when you don't have a lot of time. There's always a party or something going on. *Colgate University*

I've never worked so hard in my life. We were forever fundraising or doing some charity thing and someone was always griping about how it *should* have been done. *Michigan State University*

It's a great network during and after college. I have fraternity brothers all over the country. Someone's always got a father or an uncle who can open a door for you. *Colgate University*

I don't think it's worth it. If you're worried about networking and resumes, get out in the community and meet people, get involved in a research project. That's likely to be more helpful in the long run. *Aquinas College*

Sometimes it gets to be too much. You're always worried about your "image." Someone always wants to know, "Who did you go out with?" "What did you wear?" "Who was there?" "Why aren't you doing this or that?" *Indiana University*

Greeks always know what's happening on campus, which courses are good, who's the best prof, job openings, parties. All that, *plus* test files! *Ohio State University*

What's the "Rush?"

I pledged the first house I walked into my first semester and spent a lot of time washing dishes and scrubbing floors before I figured out that it wasn't the place for me. Don't rush your first semester. Get to *know* guys from different fraternities and what's going on in them.

Senior, Accounting, Indiana University

Forget which house is "cool" or who has the best "national." Look for people you're comfortable with. If you have to act like something you're not just to fit in, it's not worth it.

Sophomore, Premed, Cornell University

My best friend didn't get a bid . . . so I didn't accept mine. By the end of the term she had a boyfriend and I hardly saw her. I ended up wishing I was in a sorority. You need to do what's best for *you*.

Junior, English, Indiana University

Pledging is like taking an additional four credits, at least. Plan your schedule accordingly.

Senior, Economics, University of Connecticut

Some fraternities make it impossible to get decent grades while you're pledging. **My G.P.A. never recovered.** If grades are your priority, make sure there's at least *some* value placed on academics in the house you're pledging.

Senior, Business, Northern Illinois University

BEWARE of Greeks

Greek at one school can be totally different from Greek at another. Ours is big on parties, but sports, academics, and community service are big too. At my brother's school, **the houses are trashed and so are the guys** most of the time. Their idea of sports is playing SEGA while smoking a joint.

Senior, Marketing, Ohio University

If a chapter has a high GPA, a student's grades go up ... if low, they go down.

The biggest use of drugs and alcohol is in the fraternities.

Junior, Geology, Arizona State University

Everyone hazes. It ranges from mild harassment to perverted and dangerous. Unfortunately you never know which until you're in the middle of it. By then, not only have you invested a huge amount of time, but you also don't want to look like a wimp by bailing out.

Sophomore, Advertising, University of Florida

After making it through a whole semester of pledging, our "I" Week, otherwise known as **"HELL WEEK,"** turned out to be two weeks—one for the official initiation and another for the "unofficial" one. The fact that no one was allowed to study during either, forced two of us to decide whether we wanted to be Sigma Chi's or M.D.'s . . ..

Junior, Biology, University of Michigan

"**College was what I wanted to do socially, not academically. I wish I'd taken it more seriously.**"

Graduate, English, Rutgers University

Ah Ha!

Words from the
wise . . .

Going to college was for my parents. It wasn't until
I realized I was there for *myself* that I got serious.
Unfortunately, that was pretty late in the game.
Somehow it has to become *your* goal . . .
the sooner, the better.

Graduate, Supply Chain Management, Michigan State University

College was just the next thing to do . . . and I could play soccer. At some point, it occurred to me that I really LIKED to learn and LIKED to talk to people about what they'd learned. I never knew that . . ..

Senior, Sociology, University of Colorado

I wish I hadn't put so much pressure on myself. There were so many things going on that I missed. I should have relaxed, enjoyed it more, and done things because I wanted to, not because it looked good on a resumé.

Graduate, English, Indiana University

Lifetime value of a college diploma: $1,535,100.

College is the *time* to struggle to learn a formula or a concept . . . it's *supposed* to be hard. That's how you learn to think, to problem-solve. Your boss probably won't be as lenient or as helpful as your professors.

Graduate, Finance and Business, Notre Dame

Geez, where do I start . . .? There are *so many* things I wish I'd done . . . I could kick myself for not realizing that college was probably the *only* time I'd have the freedom *and* the opportunity to explore options and try a lot of different things. After you graduate, it's all about paying bills . . . there's no time and no opportunity for much else.

Graduate, Marketing, University of Wisconsin

If I end up never being a biologist, I still wouldn't trade my life in college. I learned so much about who I am . . . what makes me succeed and what makes me fail. **It was an exploration of *me* . . .**

Graduate, Biology, MIT

"Not everyone gets where they're going the same way."

WHAT IT'S ALL ABOUT . . .

You don't "get it" when you're in college. It's not about what you major in or which classes you take . . . you won't remember most of them anyway. It's really about learning to *think* and to *communicate*. *Wherever* you end up, you'll need to be able to analyze and solve problems—to figure out what needs to be done and do it! "Doing it" takes being organized, having the ability to express yourself effectively, and a lot of other skills you didn't realize you were learning in some of those "boring, senseless" courses. You can definitely scam your way through college without developing those skills . . . a lot of kids do . . . but in the long run, you're only limiting *yourself*. And believe me, that can make your first job a little scary.

Graduate, Marketing, Ohio University

I have like thirty days until I graduate and I'm so depressed . . . It took me until my senior year to appreciate the fact that I can walk right out my door and learn anything I want . . . **it's all right here.** College puts you in touch with so much . . . so many kinds of people, so many opportunities to try things. I'm more accepting, more open . . .. It takes every college student a while to figure things out, but I'd definitely say, "Take advantage of the fact that you're there. Enjoy."

Senior, Human Development, University of Connecticut

"#*@%!!!, where was this book when I needed it?!?"

Senior, Business, University of Michigan

SHARE YOUR TIPS

There's nothing better than the voice of experience. If you have any "hot tips" or words of wisdom you'd like to share, please do at

styler@voyager.net
FAX: (517) 487-0888

Front Porch Press
P.O. Box 234
Haslett, MI 48840